A Place to Worship

A Place to Worship

AFRICAN AMERICAN CAMP MEETINGS IN THE CAROLINAS

Minuette Floyd

THE UNIVERSITY OF SOUTH CAROLINA PRESS

Published by the University of South Carolina Press
Columbia, South Carolina 29208

www.sc.edu/uscpress

Manufactured in Canada

27 26 25 24 23 22 21 20 19 18   10 9 8 7 6 5 4 3 2 1

Library of Congress Cataloging-in-Publication Data
can be found at http://catalog.loc.gov/.

ISBN: 978-1-61117-887-6 (cloth)
ISBN: 978-1-61117-888-3 (paperback)
ISBN: 978-1-61117-889-0 (ebook)

FRONTISPIECE: Alin Rigby, Shady Grove Camp ground, 2014

Put off thy shoes from off thy feet: for the place where thou standest is holy ground.

Exodus 3:5

CONTENTS

FOREWORD

"A picture is worth a thousand words." So goes a popular adage. If this axiom is true, it begs the question: what happens if a picture is accompanied by a "thousand words"? One obvious answer may be that the idea under consideration suffers overkill. Another possibility would be that the additional information embellishes the work more. This latter scenario is precisely what occurs in this collection of photographs, titled *A Place to Worship: African American Camp Meetings in the Carolinas.* In her treatment of the camp-meeting phenomenon, Dr. Minuette Floyd provides a provocative portfolio of photographs and establishes a context for this subject matter. She further frames the camp-meeting dynamic with delightfully written passages. These passages provide personal and historical perspectives and offer a captivating literary and visual experience. In the narrative readers are extended a familiarity and kinship that places them in the midst of the experiences of the participants, Dr. Floyd included.

That Minuette Floyd is a photographer of some skill was evident in her works exhibited in previous venues, and her skills are manifest in this volume. While each of the photographs collected here speak with the power of a thousand words, the addition of the narrative imposes clarity on the camp-meeting experience that may otherwise be lost. Dr. Floyd achieves this by weaving her personal and familial experiences with historical annotations and first-hand anecdotal accounts from camp-meeting participants. By doing so, the author paints a sensitive portrait that strikes a delicate balance between the art of photographic documentation and the sensitivity of grassroots storytelling. She carries readers with her on a voyage that not only introduces the world of the camp meeting but also provides a vantage point that makes her fellow journeyers feel like both observer and participant. Some attempts to do this fall short of this mark because of a tendency to be trite and clichéd given the nature of the subject matter. Dr. Floyd avoids this trap by establishing a framework that is subtle in its combination of intent, content, and context. These variables serve as mitigating factors, which allow readers to embrace the notion of the camp-meeting dynamic with the simultaneous infusion of their own experiences.

An achievement of this magnitude is a noteworthy accomplishment, because the experience becomes more than slices of moments in the mind of one person. It rises to a level of cultural and humanistic significance and places us more in touch with one another through shared values. This spiritual connection is at the core of what one aspires to when seeking a sense of belonging. Whether that feeling comes via a single photograph, the proverbial thousand words, or a combination of both, in this instance Minuette Floyd delivers.

TERRY K. HUNTER

ACKNOWLEDGMENTS

My journey to document the African American camp-meeting experience has been a phenomenal time of reminiscing and learning. I have met so many wonderful friends along the way. Thanks to my parents, Aline and Raeford Byers, who introduced me to camp meeting at a young age. Although you have moved on, I will forever remember the important life lessons that you instilled in me. To my brother, Allen, and sister-in-law, Debra, thank you for inviting me back to camp meeting; who could have known the impact that my return would have on my life, and now, fifteen years later, I am still uncovering its rich history and sacred stories. Thanks to my wonderful nieces and nephews—Asya, Ariel, Tia, Allen, and Tony—and to the other young campers who participated in my disposable camera project so that I could see camp meeting through their lens. Thanks to my sister, Rae, and brother-in-law, Audwin Helton, owners of Spatial Data Integrations, Inc., for their assistance in designing the camp-meeting map.

Thank you to my mother-in-law, Alice Carter, for your support and confidence in me. I am immensely grateful for the support of my husband, Reggie, and for his patience and encouragement. Thanks for overlooking the pile of books and papers that accumulated on tables and floors while I worked on this project. And thank you to Dr. Cynthia Colbert, Nina DeCordova, and Deloris Pringle, who encouraged me and provided editorial support when I needed it most.

Thanks to the University of South Carolina and former dean, College of Arts and Sciences, Mary Anne Fitzpatrick who provided grant opportunities for which I was able to apply. This funding assisted me in bringing this documentary to fruition. Thanks to the National Endowment for the Arts, the S.C. Arts Commission, and the S.C. Humanities Council for financial support during the many phases of this research and documentation.

I don't know how to begin to express my gratitude to all of my camp-meeting family; I love you all and am so grateful for you. I could not have done this without you. I will always remember all of my camp-meeting family and friends who have passed on since I began this project. "When I've gone the last mile of the way, there is joy that awaits me," goes lines from "The Last Mile of the Way," by Sam Cooke, my father's favorite gospel singer. I grew up hearing Dad sing this song at home, at church, and at the campground.

SHADY GROVE

Mama Alin Rigby and her daughter,
Patricia Charthern
The Jerome Jones family
The Beatrice-Elmore family
The Jones family
Reverend Dr. John Elliott
The family of Mr. Shell Johnson

TUCKER'S GROVE

Lewis McLean
Mr. and Mrs. Jerry Ross and family
Reverend Albert Perkins, Sr. and family

MCKENZIE'S GROVE

The late Mrs. Faydene Jones
The late Mr. Isaiah Springs and family

MOTT'S GROVE

Mrs. Harriett Gabriel and family
Mr. Kelsey McCleave and family
Ronni McCombs and family

ST. PAUL

Alfred Calvin
Mr. and Mrs. Herbert Gardner and family
Barbara Felder and family
Shirley Brown and family
The late Mr. Richard Neal and family
The Lennerd Mack family

CAMP WELFARE

Viola Hall and family
Dorothy Stewart and family
Shirley Kennedy and family
The late Mrs. Malvina Moore

MOUNT CARMEL

The late Darryl T. Murphy and family
Reverend Bennie Stinson and family

I would also like to acknowledge the members of the boards of trustees at each of the campgrounds. Their hard work in the continuous preservation and upkeep of the grounds is important for future generations.

Last and not least: I ask forgiveness of all of those who have supported me and this project over the years and whose names I failed to mention.

INTRODUCTION

In Dr. Minuette Floyd's *A Place To Worship: African American Camp Meetings in the Carolinas* we have an opportunity to witness a spiritual and social gathering that has spanned generations. In the first half of the nineteenth century enslaved African Americans were delegated to adjacent meetings as white masters held their own worship related camp meetings. With reconstruction former slaves continued the practice and today the African American camp meeting is synonymous with family, community, place, and spirituality. Floyd's research reveals the role camp meetings played in the salvation of generations emerging from repression, Jim Crow, and segregation.

Through images and research, *A Place To Worship* helps us visualize the open sky of the meeting and the covered arbor central to the gathering. The arbor is where we find sounds of preaching, music, and a congregation. Its rhythm continues through the raw, cabin-like structures called tents surrounding the arbor. Handed down from one generation to the next, the tents see family after family greeting one another and renewing friendships on the good ground that is the weeklong meeting. Part holiday, part revival, part family reunion, camp meeting sites are still tucked away in rural fields and governed by common purpose and familiar rules. They are alive and well.

In *A Place To Worship* Floyd revisits childhood memories of that good ground while producing a scholarly investigation linking historical background with her own photographic documentation. Before she started grade school, her parents brought Minuette and her three siblings to camp meetings in Lincoln and Catawba counties in North Carolina. It was the social gathering of the year, a time to participate in a larger reality. Recognizing its cultural significance, she began research and documentation of camp meetings in 1996 that continues today.

With *A Place to Worship* Floyd has established a new dialogue about this tradition often hidden from our virtual world. Media as we know it is not part of the camp experience. It is rediscovering individuals and families coming together to rekindle childhood excitement alongside worship. This book helps us recognize the camp meeting as a folk tradition with historical and social significance. It might help us understand more fully aspects of a cultural divide that still impacts our communities.

Camp meetings represent a communal destination designed for worship, food, music, and close proximity. We can see this in Floyd's images that bring *A Place To Worship* to life. There is the bare light bulb that hangs in the midst of the arbor or a busy kitchen that consumes all the space within a family's tent. These are authentic symbols of spirituality and humanity. They describe qualities of expression and character that cannot be put into words.

Floyd's photographs of worship services, interiors, families, and structures exist as a major exhibition waiting to happen. The black and white format creates a world that is both factual and something we can only imagine. They help us feel the sense of place that Minuette Floyd has experienced. They remind us that there is still a reason to celebrate an open sky and a field full of kindred spirits.

TOM STANLEY

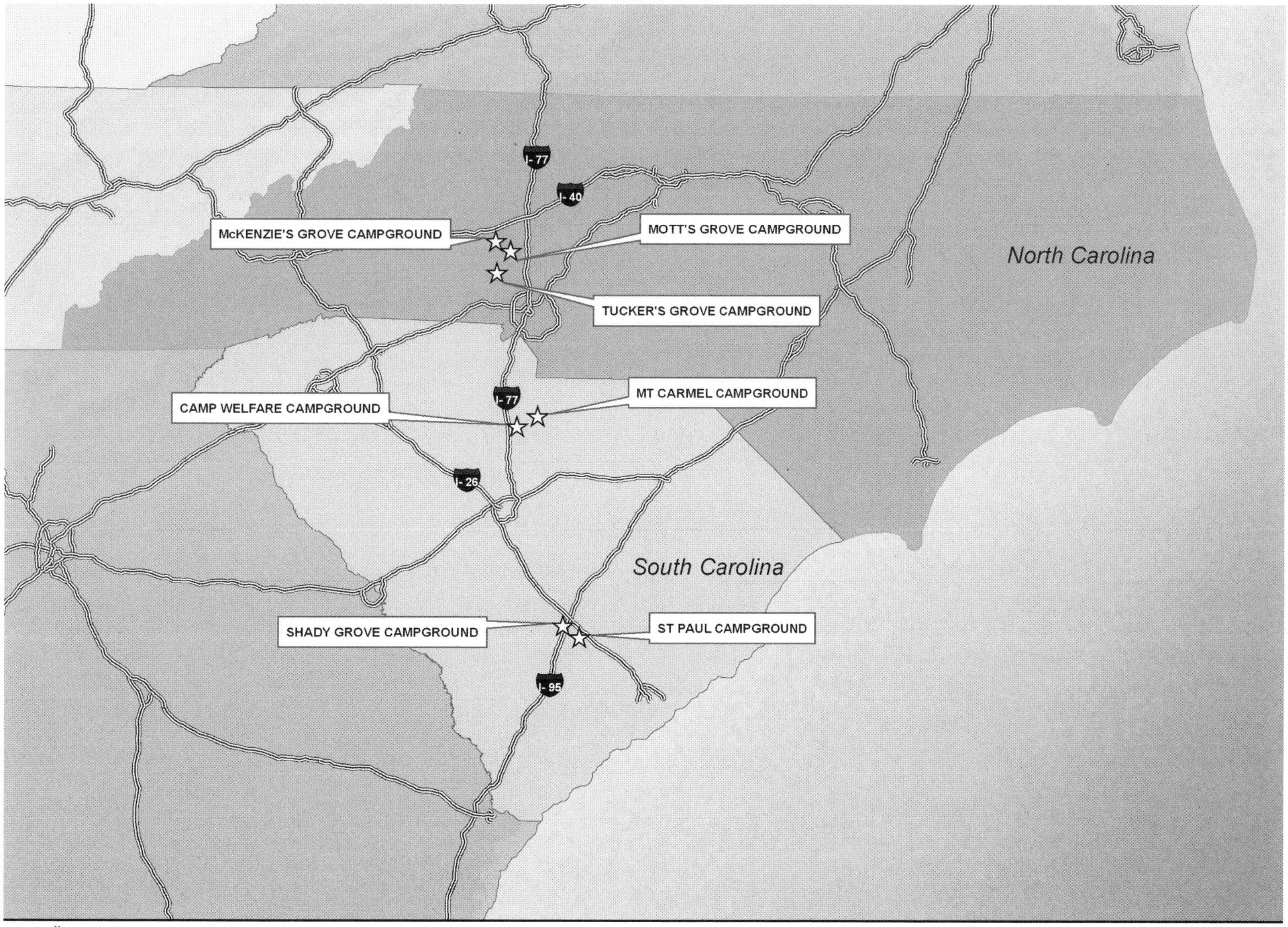

Campgrounds

Miles 0 12.5 25 50 75 100

© SDI

Old Sign, Tucker's Grove Camp Meeting, 2006

1

My Story

In August 1996, I traveled down a country road in the sticky summer heat and stepped onto the grounds of Tucker's Grove Camp Meeting. Surprisingly little had changed. The makeshift wooden sign that had been in place for twenty-five years or more still stood as the first indication that we had arrived. The old concession stands still sprawled casually around the unpaved entryway, their wooden slats worn grey by the elements. And the jubilant crowd, many dressed in their Sunday best, still stirred up little explosions of dust as they rushed to throw their arms around old friends.

I recognized one of the original concessions too, a snowball stand that Mrs. Emma Sloan and her children had run for the past fifty years. And there was Mrs. Sloan herself—a little stooped, a little gray—serving a line of eager young customers. Her family's photo stand, opened in 1958, stood nearby. The Rivens family was still there too, serving supper and snow cones just as they had done for many years. A hand-printed sign at Mrs. Sloan's elbow told me that snowballs were now a dollar each. I remembered buying them for twenty-five cents!

Minuette Floyd, Shady Grove Camp Meeting, 2014

CHILDHOOD MEMORIES

And I remembered so much more. When I grew up near Charlotte, North Carolina, in the 1960s, camp meetings were a regular part of my life. On Saturday or Sunday afternoons in the fall, my parents, Aline and Raeford Byers, would take our whole family to Tucker's Grove. We also attended Mott's Grove, McKenzie's Grove, and Morrow's Chapel—camp-meeting grounds in North Carolina that originally were Methodist or African Methodist Episcopal but now often have an interdenominational flavor.

Tuckers Grove Grounds, 2011

We always looked forward to traveling in my dad's Buick, with its wide, slick seats and stylish fins. My older sister, Raefette, my younger brother, Allen, and I would automatically climb into the back—we were close in age. Our sister Suzette, seven years younger than me, would sit up front on my mom's lap. My dad's cousin Gert, a very kind woman in her late sixties, often traveled with us, riding in back with the older kids.

This was before the prevalence of fast food restaurants, so we always ate well before traveling the back roads for more than an hour through farmland and heavily forested areas. Then we parked across the street from the campground in a large dirt field, so that cars would not block us in. People who lived in the surrounding neighborhoods often walked to camp meeting, though car traffic was heavy too. Our dad would lead the way across the street, grasping our hands tightly. I remember lots of big silver bumpers and out-of-state license plates and scurrying three or four steps for each of my dad's long strides.

Emma Sloan at Tucker's Grove Camp Meeting, 2014

My family, left to right: Raefette Allen, my mom, Aline, and Minuette with cousin Gert, circa 1969

THE CROWDS

There was always a large crowd of people near the entrance, hugging and catching up. Despite the dust, women wore colorful hats and dresses, and some wore high heels too. Many of the men wore dark suits with white shirts, hats, and shiny dress shoes. When camp attendees stopped at a store on their way home, people who saw their nice shoes all dusty would guess that they had been to the campgrounds.

Just inside the entrance, then as now, were the concession stands. There were snowballs and popcorn and bright candy apples lined up on trays. Fried chicken and fish dinners were served alongside green beans, cornbread, and macaroni and cheese. There were pies and cakes and hot dogs and hamburgers too. Other stands sold small toys, and there were photo stands where you could have your picture taken in a large, wicker, fan-backed chair with a colorful, often exotic landscape as a background.

We children stayed close to our parents to avoid getting lost in the crowd. We knew not to ask for anything from the concession stands—that would come later. For now it was all about spying the familiar faces of family, friends, and acquaintances. There was always a great feeling of celebration. Some people may not have seen one another since last year's camp meeting, especially if they lived in another state.

As we moved through the crowd, my dad shook nearly every hand—he never met a stranger—and proudly introduced us all. Sometimes he would strike up long conversations with people we assumed were old friends, then tell us they had just met. As the adults caught up with one another, we children waited politely. Our eyes kept rolling back toward the concession stands, where, in time, we'd have some wonderful choices to make.

Our family always went right to the arbor, where the religious services were held. But first we needed to walk through a narrow passage, just large enough for a car to drive through. On either side were the "tents." That name has carried over from the early days of makeshift canvas structures, but actually these are small, hand-built dwellings, usually of unpainted wood, where families stay during religious services. Squeezed close together in a large square around the arbor, the tents might have rustic cracks from the way the wood has aged, and they all have front porches facing the arbor. Waving to people on the porches, we could now hear singing and the sounds of preaching or testifying up ahead.

THE ARBOR

The arbor at Tucker's Grove is more than one hundred years old. It has no walls, just sturdy posts and a system of trusses holding up a big tin roof. The construction is vintage: wood was cut precisely, interlocked, and held together with pegs instead of nails. The roof is low too, so tall people have to bend a bit. The ushers, usually men in dapper suits, would greet us at the entrance. Each had a fistful of paper fans in case anyone got overheated or overcome by the Spirit. If someone were praying, we would wait until they finished before going under the arbor.

The arbor was always crowded with a couple hundred people, so we usually sat near the back. Though the main pulpit was elevated, we children often could not see it because of adults sitting in front of us. Sometimes, too, the ladies would have on large-brimmed hats. But we could hear people spontaneously testifying or breaking into song. Eventually we could hear the choir's hymns and the pastor's sermon. When we were younger, our parents would let us take turns sitting in their laps so that we could have a clearer view.

We grew up during a time when children truly respected adults. It was not unusual for us to sit quietly on the old wooden benches for up to two hours. A bee might fly through the arbor, or we might spy something interesting in the fresh sawdust beneath our feet. Then our parents would tap us on the leg to keep us focused on the service. Our thoughts never drifted far from the snow cones, though. And sometimes we just fell asleep, leaning on our mom's or dad's lap.

Eventually the whole crowd stood for the benediction. Dad looked all around for familiar faces—people we could hug and catch up with as soon as the service ended. Then we would greet people on the porches of the tents and greet others by the concession stands. Finally we children would enjoy a few glorious moments choosing some sweets or a new toy such as a stuffed animal or cap gun.

By now my dad, always a stickler for time, would be looking at his watch. Maybe the issue was getting home before nightfall or staying ahead of a thunderstorm. Back in the Buick, sticky and satisfied, one child laid her head down in Cousin Gert's lap. Then the others would lean together, and Dad would drive us all home in the gathering dark.

FAST FORWARD

In 1996, when I stepped back onto the grounds at Tucker's Grove, every one of these memories came flooding back. Of course the grounds looked smaller—that always happens as you grow. But plenty of people still recognized me, including high school classmates, because the place was still a magnet and a staple for the community.

A REVOLUTION UNFOLDS

Now I walked beside my adult brother and his wife, whose family has always "tented" there. Now I watched their children's eyes dart back toward the snow cones. But as we made our way to the arbor, several older people shouted out, "You Raeford's daughter?" Of course they knew who I was—I have my dad's eyes.

Leaving the campground that evening, I noticed a man taking photographs. I thought to myself, I have *got* to capture this tradition. How little I knew at that time! I had no idea that camp meetings took place outside North Carolina, and no idea either that there were white camp meetings throughout the South. But the inspiration had taken hold, and there was no turning back.

THE JOURNEY BEGINS

Within a couple of days of arriving home—I'd recently moved to Columbia, South Carolina—I began the research. But I could not find much written about African American camp meetings. Eventually my search led me to an 1872 issue of *Harper's Weekly* that consisted of an image and article describing a Caucasian person's discovery of and fascination with what was called "a Negro camp meeting"; the article was extremely stereotyping. It made me wonder how I could best describe camp meetings to someone who has no prior knowledge of the tradition and no sense of its importance.

Thus began my quest to document this history accurately. I wanted to provide a contemporary examination of African American camp meetings and highlight the people who play key roles. I wanted to capture people involved in rituals and sacred activities. I also wanted to record the history of camp meetings from the mouths of the elder attendees for future generations and their families.

Over the next year, I became so enamored with camp meetings that I began mentioning them to people in South Carolina. Most of them knew nothing about the tradition. But a handful of people knew exactly what I was talking about. They introduced me to others, who graciously introduced me to others. As people invited me to their campgrounds, into their tents and homes, and into their hearts, I began to understand the project's rich potential.

Little did I know that this was the beginning of a fifteen-year journey. Eventually it involved developing deep relationships at three campgrounds in North Carolina and four in South Carolina, all Methodist or African Methodist Episcopal. At times I have been asked which camp meeting I like the best. My response is always that I love them equally.

In fact this project has been a labor of love since the beginning. It has also been a deep dive into my own family heritage. My parents, who were such important figures in my early experience of the campgrounds, have both passed away since I began my journey.

The Negro Camp Meeting, *Harper's Weekly*, 1872

CAPTURING THE LIGHT

About halfway through this long effort to document the campgrounds, I started noticing a recurring symbol in my photographs: bare lightbulbs like the ones that hang from sockets underneath the tin roofs of arbors. I might have captured a lightbulb flaring above the pastor's head as he scaled the heights of a sermon, or one glowing across a dusty path to welcome weary travelers at night.

Though it took me years to notice the way my camera gravitated to this symbol, it immediately made sense. I was trying to capture the feeling of spiritual illumination—the core of the experience at every campground.

My Dad, Raeford Byers, Tucker's Grove Camp Meeting, 2004

Raeford Byers was born February 6, 1929, near Charlotte, North Carolina. He never had an opportunity to meet his father. During the Great Depression, his mother struggled so hard to support him and his brother that one day she found herself walking up and down the street looking for someone financially stable enough to take the boys in. When Raeford was four years old, Julia and Green Byers took him in. They later adopted him.

Dad always went to church, and camp meetings were the core of his spiritual life. He loved music, and he loved singing. I remember him playing Sam Cooke and the Soul Stirrers on the record player and then singing those same songs beautifully under the arbor.

When I began this project in 1996, Dad was still driving himself to camp meetings. I often met him there. My mom's health had declined, and she was now living in a nursing home, so he loved having the company. Then, as Dad got older, I began to drive home first, and he rode with me to the campgrounds. My sense of direction was always challenged in rural areas, so this gave him the chance to teach me all the old back roads.

Dad's last camp meeting was in 2006 at McKenzie's Grove. His face lit up as we drove onto the grounds. He still wore dress slacks, a hat, and the watch that had kept our lives so orderly. Fragile as he was, he still loped around the grounds, shaking every hand and carrying on long conversations.

Dad passed away in 2008. Thinking about him recently, I realized that even though you grow up in camp meeting, you also have to grow into it as an adult. I am deeply grateful that Dad was there for both phases of my camp-meeting journey. "Train a child in the way he should go and when he is old, he will not turn from it."[1]

Corine Jones Benson, 88 years old. "I can remember only missing three years of camp meeting." Mount Carmel Camp Meeting, 2006

SO LITTLE CHANGE

Over the fifteen years I have been documenting camp meetings, I have observed only minor changes in the campgrounds. I have seen concession stands come and go. Some tents have been torn down, including the preacher's tent at Mott's Grove. Other tents have had rooms or a porch or a second story added. Still others have been totally rebuilt. One rebuilt the arbor. Tucker's Grove now has a red brick sign and also a large rock garden near the arbor surrounded by a flower garden. Six of the campgrounds featured in this book are listed on the National Register of Historic Places. Four of them have had historical markers placed on site, and three had accompanying ceremonial services, which I was able to witness firsthand.

The campgrounds are truly a mystical place. They are set aside from everyday life so that attendees have time to reflect on how good God has been to them. That happens in heightened moments of worship, when we clap our hands and stomp our feet more expressively than we might in a modern, air-conditioned church. It happens at peaceful moments too, just sitting on a porch looking up through the branches of a tall oak tree. People talk about heaven, but on the grounds you really feel that there is not much space between you and the sky.

As children, we could not understand this, but we could see it evidenced in the reactions of people who shouted under the arbor during a heartfelt sermon. We could also feel the powerful embrace of the campground community. Here families wandered easily from porch to porch—sharing stories, admiring new babies, mourning family members and friends who had passed away. Here children played under the watchful eyes of the people running the concession stands, who saw them grow from birth to marriage and beyond.

All of this continued to happen at camp meetings even as the sense of community was beginning to ebb from our daily lives. The Carolinas have seen enormous changes over the past few decades, as our small towns became suburbs and the increasingly hectic pace of life tore us away from our neighbors. But in this strange new century, camp meetings still offer a secure retreat. They still offer, as the old song says, a rock in a weary land.

MY EQUIPMENT

My photo documentation began with the use of my Canon AE-1 Program film camera. I was always equipped with several rolls of black and white film. In 2005 I bought my first digital camera, which made it possible to shoot and discard an unlimited number of images. Over the years I have used a Nikon D 70 digital camera and most recently a Nikon D7000 camera. I have also used a variety of video cameras to capture live footage. With changes in camera equipment, I can now use my camera to capture video footage.

Crowned Glory, Shady Grove Camp Meeting, 2007. Neomia Coger (sitting on left) travels from Florida every year for camp meeting. She enjoys time with her family and friends.

Arbor, Tucker's Grove Camp Meeting, 2014

Dad, Tucker's Grove Camp Meeting, 2001

Reverend Dr. John H. Elliott, pastor of Trinity, St. Mark, and Shady Grove United Methodist Churches, has served as the host pastor for the past 22 years. The final Sunday of camp meeting, known as "Big Sunday," begins with Sunday school, prayer service, devotion and six sermons by different pastors that last into the evening. Shady Grove Camp Meeting, 2007

Young man, Shady Grove Camp Meeting, 2007

Jerry Ross and great grandson, Caius, Mott's Grove Camp Meeting, 2013

2

Back Then

In the nineteenth century, camp meetings flourished throughout the United States. They were a major social and religious institution, with large numbers of people often traveling great distances to take part. "The camp meeting," says historian Dickson Bruce, "was a major social event of frontier life, inasmuch as it offered an unparalleled occasion for all the people in a territory to gather for several days of social activity, unencumbered by a need to work."[1]

Camp meetings originally sprang from the work of John Wesley, a British minister considered the father of American Methodism. As early as 1739, Wesley began preaching in the open air in the rural, wooded regions of England as a way to reach people unlikely to attend church. In both England and America, this practice continued among Methodists, Baptists, Presbyterians, and other denominations as a means of gathering followers and converting sinners through spiritual transformation.[2]

Bishop Frances Asbury, head of the American Methodist church, arrived in the United States in the 1770s and preached tirelessly, indoors and out, for more than forty-five years. Riding roughly six thousand miles per year, often surviving on little more than beef jerky, Asbury was once so ill that he had to strap himself to his horse to continue traveling.[3] The bishop's extraordinary eloquence, dedication, and passion played an instrumental role in the spread of camp meetings in America.[4]

BLACK HARRY

Early accounts of black camp-meeting leadership point to Harry Hoosier, known as Black Harry, who was born into slavery in Fayetteville, North Carolina, in 1750.

By 1780 Hoosier was a freedman working as Francis Asbury's traveling companion and servant as they moved about on horseback. Later he proved himself as a colleague and began preaching to slaves while Asbury preached to white people. Eventually Hoosier was acclaimed as one of the greatest preachers in America, often speaking along with Asbury on the itinerant trail from the Carolinas up to New England.

Hoosier preached the religious philosophy of John Wesley, and it is speculated that he also preached about freedom and justice. His popular and powerful sermons were embraced by people of both races. In fact, Asbury wrote, the best way to draw a crowd was to announce that Hoosier would preach. He admitted that Hoosier drew larger crowds than he did.[5]

SLAVES ENCOURAGED

Research on African American participation in early camp meetings is very limited. We do know that whites were encouraged to bring slaves to the meetings because it was thought that "religious instruction would help make them servile and obedient."[6]

Sometimes black and white people worshipped together at camp meetings. Blacks might, for example, stand in the narrow aisles underneath the arbor close to the preacher. At that time men sat on benches on one side of the arbor and women on another side. Presumably the slaves were similarly divided. At other times slaves were encouraged to hold their own gatherings on the backside of the campground. In at least one instance—Rock Springs Campground in Catawba County, North Carolina—separate arbors were built for whites and blacks.[7]

The growth of camp meetings organized specifically for African Americans is sparsely documented, and often the documentation is contradictory. But the lack of a clear written record is not surprising. The arbors where African American services were held were called "brush arbors," to indicate their rustic location, or "hush arbors" to indicate that they were secret and especially sacred. This tradition lingers to the present day, with African American camp meetings still difficult to trace because they are usually not advertised outside their own community.

Grover Colbert, Mount Carmel, 2012

"I remember when there was no electricity and flambeaus were hung on poles. Gas was poured into a jar that had a rag in it, and then it was lit." Grover Colbert, Mount Carmel, September 8, 2012.

MEMORY AS HISTORY

Much of what we know of early African American camp meetings, then, comes from oral histories—and much of that is similar to the white camp-meeting tradition. African American meetings were held annually at harvest time, though they could take place throughout the warm season. Most took place between July and October, when people could leave behind the responsibility of farming.

The choice of a site was very important. Most African American camp meetings took place in rural, sparsely populated areas, where churches were either too small to accommodate the number of people in attendance or did not exist at all. Water and pasture land were needed to support a large crowd, as well as a place to park wagons and carriages and a place for horses and mules to graze. The site was usually located in a large grove where smaller trees could be cleared and larger trees could provide a sheltering canopy.

OUR OWN LAND

Initially most camp meetings were held on borrowed land. Ultimately all the established campgrounds received gifts of land or purchased it at a nominal fee. Most property transfers involved an explicit agreement that the land would be used only for religious purposes.

Some grounds took on the name of the person from whom the land was obtained. For example participants at Mott's Grove still talk about John J. Mott, the elderly local doctor who donated the first piece of land to African American neighbors he found worshipping outdoors shortly after the Civil War.

Caesar Wolfe, a former slave, started the Shady Grove camp meeting just after the Civil War. Wolfe lived in coastal South Carolina near rice fields owned by a farmer named S. M. Knight. One summer Knight's crop was threatened by an approaching storm. Wolfe quickly persuaded other former slaves to help him gather the rice before it was destroyed. After the storm the grateful farmer gave Wolfe and his neighbors a piece of land to be used exclusively for religious purposes.

However the campgrounds were initially acquired, they were all too small to accommodate modern needs, including cars and recreational campers. Most of the

Maggie Brace, Camp Welfare, 2013

"We came on a mule-drawn wagon and tied the mules up in the woods. We brought everything we needed: hay to feed the mules and a straw mattress to provide comfort while we slept. We'd bring sweet potato pies and teacakes in a pillowcase. It wouldn't spoil. We didn't have refrigerators then. We'd walk down to the spring to get water in a bucket." Maggie Brace, Camp Welfare, August 23, 2013.

Ceasar Wolfe Historical Center, Shady Grove 2013

campgrounds have been expanded over time through subsequent purchases. (See Appendix A for a brief history of each campground.)

GATHERING FROM AFAR

Gathering at the campgrounds from miles around, participants brought everything they would need for two to three weeks. Older people still remember their parents piling mattresses on top of mule-drawn wagons. Livestock might be hitched behind the wagon and live chickens hauled in a crate. The late Mr. Isaiah Springs, born in 1922 and was chair of McKenzie's Campground, remembers bringing a hatchet and chopping block to dispatch chickens for Saturday dinner. And when a family brought their icebox, it was literally that—including a block of ice so big that it could keep food cool for days. Some campers remember the iceman who delivered the ice to the grounds on designated days.

Early camp-meeting preachers were called circuit riders and traveled great distances to reach the sites. Certain preachers were widely known, and participants flocked to hear them based on word of mouth. The roads leading to the groves literally overflowed with people on horseback, on foot, and traveling in wagons. Some of these travelers were just lonely or curious. But most came excited and anxious to hear the word of God. Celebrating their release from the toil and isolation of farmwork, they gathered to commune in nature under the stars, to renew their spirits, and to fulfill a deep and abiding need.

Viola Hall, Camp Welfare, 2009

"We had to sleep on the floor, and I was scared of snakes coming up in them cracks. But we still want to get to the campground so bad. My mama never would come till Friday, till camp meeting almost be over. But we want to get to the campground. So after I got married, I started coming on Wednesday when camp meeting started." Viola Hall, Camp Welfare, August 25, 2006.

BIRTH TO DEATH

With people staying on the campgrounds for weeks at a time, life continued its usual rhythm. Elders might pass away and be mourned and buried. Babies might be born too. Margaret Gaither-Talford tells the story of her parents' being caught at Camp Welfare in a fierce rainstorm, with the roads too muddy to make it home. Midwives brought her into the world in a leaky tent near the arbor, with women standing around her laboring mother holding umbrellas. Every seven years Gaither-Talford still celebrates her birthday on the grounds.[8]

With crowds sometimes numbering in the thousands, misbehavior might take place. People could, for example, sneak in liquor and become unruly at night. At the Mount Carmel campground in Lancaster, North Carolina, there was a big tree near the entrance where troublemakers were handcuffed until the local paddy wagon arrived to take them away.[9] Shady Grove campground once had a jail on the property. If any of the camp participants acted improperly, they would be locked up. If they could not pay the fine, they were sent to the Saint George County Jail.[10]

Since the mysterious beginnings of African American camp meetings in the nineteenth century, human life—pious and impious, mournful and exhilarating—has continued to unfold under the sheltering trees. Some campgrounds have flourished due to auspicious locations and strong local leadership. Others have almost succumbed to fire, vandalism, or other happenstance, and loyal campers have had to rebuild them. Many African American campgrounds are more than 145 years old and are still going strong today.

Arbor, Camp Welfare, 2002

Time to Commune, Harriette Gabriel and daughter Marion Ross,
Mott's Grove, 2014

Old Arbor, St. Paul, 2006

New Arbor, St. Paul, 2011

Old Rules Sign, Tucker's Grove, 2006

New Sign, Tucker's Grove, 2011

3

Camp Life

Contemporary camp meetings are phenomenal events. People come to these spirit-filled gatherings to get to know God, to receive blessings, to pray, to testify, to reflect upon their lives, to renew old friendships, and to build new ones. For many participants the reasons for attending camp meetings have not changed since Francis Asbury and Harry Hoosier rode the circuit together. They come seeking spiritual transformation, and they are rarely disappointed. As the elders say, you never leave camp meeting the way that you came. To understand the modern camp-meeting experience, it is important to visualize the site and get the flavor of life on the grounds.

ACCOMMODATIONS

Hundreds and perhaps thousands of African American families plan their vacations around camp meeting. In many instances they travel across the United States to attend. Some people arrive in camper trailers with all the comforts of home. Empty dirt lots are often reserved for campers, whose owners pay the same fees as the people who own permanent tents.

Other than these parking lots, which are usually peripheral and somewhat hidden, the objective at most camp meetings is to preserve the cultural and historical aspects of the site. Therefore the tents and arbor maintain vernacular architectural styles reminiscent of the past.

The tents, sometimes referred to as huts or cabins, form a circular arrangement, facing inward toward the centrally located arbor where the preaching takes place. Many tents look similar on the outside—just old-fashioned, unpainted wood—but have hand-painted numbers or family names to distinguish them. Over the years some of the "tenters" have rebuilt with cinderblock so they can have a more permanent structure. However, this is dependent on the rules set by the board of trustees and is not allowed at campgrounds with a stronger focus on historic preservation.

Each year there is much work to do to prepare the tents for camp meeting. This includes everything from replacing worn boards and patching roofs to cleaning the interior, removing worn furniture, and bringing old furniture from home into the tent. When the tent is first opened, family members make sure that they get rid of spiders or even snakes that may have made the tent their home over the past year. They unpack plastic containers that have been used to store pots, pans, and bedding supplies. These responsibilities are divided among family members, and those committed to the success of the event begin driving out to the grounds weeks before camp meeting. Inside, today's tents are usually quite comfortable. They have beds, stoves, refrigerators, and living room furniture, and some even have televisions. Most have solid floors now too—unlike the dirt or sawdust floors from decades past.

Many tents have kitchen sinks for washing dishes. Toilets are located directly behind the tents (and there are also centrally located public toilets for other participants). Some camps still maintain old-fashioned outhouses, but most families now pay a rental fee to have a portable toilet brought to the grounds. Some families have bathrooms built into their tents. People bring enough clothes too, so they do not have to wash them.

Tents belong to family members and are passed down from generation to generation. They are like family portraits: each piece of wood, each door, each window reflects those who built the tent and spent time there. Sometimes a family is no longer able to maintain their tent, so they let someone else use it. There is a long waiting list of people wishing to gain access to any tents that become available. Depending on the circumstance, the family or the campground's board of trustees decides who should assume ownership.

Each campground has a board of trustees that oversees the campground, making all the important decisions about the public areas. They take on innumerable duties and responsibilities throughout the year but mainly during camp-meeting season. Over the years most of the camps have published a Policies and Procedures manual that is distributed to each tent owner. During camp meeting members of the board are available to assist tent owners and also to enforce and maintain camp rules. These trustees are responsible for collecting the annual fee that is paid for the upkeep of the campgrounds as well as the fee paid to have the electricity and water turned on prior to the start of camp meeting. The board of trustees no longer bears the sole responsibility of keeping the peace on the campgrounds. Most have assistance from the local sheriff's department, which keeps several cars parked on the periphery of the grounds, as well as from policemen taking scheduled strolls to ensure a peaceful camp experience. (See Appendix B for sample camp-meeting rules.)

FOODWAYS

Food is integral to camp meeting. When visitors first step onto a campground, the scent of burning wood mixed with the aroma of southern food quickly captures their senses. Roasted pork and fried chicken, red rice, rutabagas, sweet potatoes, corn, and greens are just a few of the foods eaten throughout the week.

Before electricity was available at the campgrounds, people prepared food communally over open fires. Once electric lights, refrigerators, and gas stoves were added to the tents, much of the cooking moved indoors and became more family oriented.

In most homes it is common to plan for a big thanksgiving food festival. At camp meeting meals may be three times the size of that holiday celebration. Over the course of the week, food is prepared for a hundred or more family members and friends. It is by far the biggest family event of the year, and a great deal of planning goes into dividing the responsibilities and devising the menus.

Most family members cook on the campgrounds. Others cook at home and bring the food. No matter what is on the menu, there is almost always a family tradition associated with it. Some families pull oversized grills to the grounds and cook everything from hot dogs to whole hogs. One day is usually set aside for seafood. People will cook crab, shrimp, and a variety of fish, including croaker, perch, flounder, spot, and trout. Anyone walking in the vicinity will hear the sizzling sound of oil as people fry fish or chicken both inside and outside the tent.

Sometimes you will see people driving through the grounds selling foods ready to be cooked. The "sweet potato man," for example, circles the grounds of Shady Grove with the back of his truck filled with sweet potatoes for sale. Or you might see Mr. Jerome Johnson selling collard greens from the back of his truck.

Some families still use heirloom cast-iron pots to deep-fry fish. Many also still cook on old-fashioned wood-burning stoves. Arthur Gardner, a lifelong participant at Saint Paul campground, has built more than three hundred "drum" or "tank" stoves at Shady

"My mom and grandmothers would bring food from home and serve it from the trunk of the car, because we weren't fortunate to have a tent at that time. That was the best-tasting food we ever ate. We did that until God blessed our parents and grandparents to be able to build a tent, and now we're still forever more eating and praising God with family and friends." Shirley Brown, Saint Paul Campground, March 10, 2015.

Grove, Saint Paul, and Indian Field campgrounds. He starts with an ice can—basically a rectangular box made of galvanized metal. Then he cuts a hole in the front, covers it with a hinged piece of tin, and lays a brick base underneath and around it.

Gardner's stoves, which each take about sixteen hours to build, can be custom-made to fit the quirky shape of each tent. As many as twenty pots can sit on one of his larger models—and in a bustling camp-meeting kitchen, cooks use every inch of that space.

SHIFTING PRIORITIES

With the focus on old-fashioned food and accommodations and with family all around, camp meetings are a natural place to hang out, catch up, and kick back. One of the ways campers use this leisure time together is to commemorate family milestones. Perhaps it is a surprise party for a young father whose birthday falls that week. Or perhaps special time is set aside to share reminiscences of a family member who passed away during

The Children of Mr. and Mrs. Sam Ross, Tucker's Grove Camp Meeting, 2014

the year. Either way, these events often take place on a large scale and touch the broader camp community. With the tragic and unexpected passing of David Ross in 2014, more than fifty family members wore T-shirts bearing his image to Tucker's Grove, then took time to honor his memory together.

This is just one example of the many ways in which camp meetings allow participants to stop the whirlwind of daily activity, look one another in the eye, and focus on things that really matter. For most participants that requires a conscious shift of priorities. Even if you're accustomed to modern comforts, at camp meeting you may have to adjust to using an outhouse. You may have to shed your iPad and iPhone and GPS too. Although some are moved out of their comfort zone, everyone makes these small sacrifices for the pleasure of seasoning food with family memories, squeezing together with cousins on a rickety porch, and prowling the same time-capsule concession stands they visited as children.

But the biggest switch in priorities is the one that allows participants to connect more freely with the divine. Louder than the murmur of the oil in the pan or the cooing of the youngest great-grandchild is the rhythm of the old spirituals floating over from the arbor in the blue twilight. That's the heartbeat you feel behind every tradition, and every encounter. It gives a mystical quality to almost everything that happens on the campground. As a young participant once said about Shady Grove, "It's a big family reunion—where God is at the center."[1]

Tents, St. Paul Camp Meeting, 2012

Tent Bedroom, Lutricia Tidwell Gaither, Camp Welfare Camp Meeting, 2007

Nellie Lofton (left) and the late Frances Smith (right) reminisce about camp meeting. Tucker's Grove Camp Meeting, 2011

Checkers. The late Robert Reed (left) and the late David Stradford (right) play checkers outside a tent. Throughout the days and the evenings, people pass the time in a variety of ways between the worship services. Mount Carmel, 2006

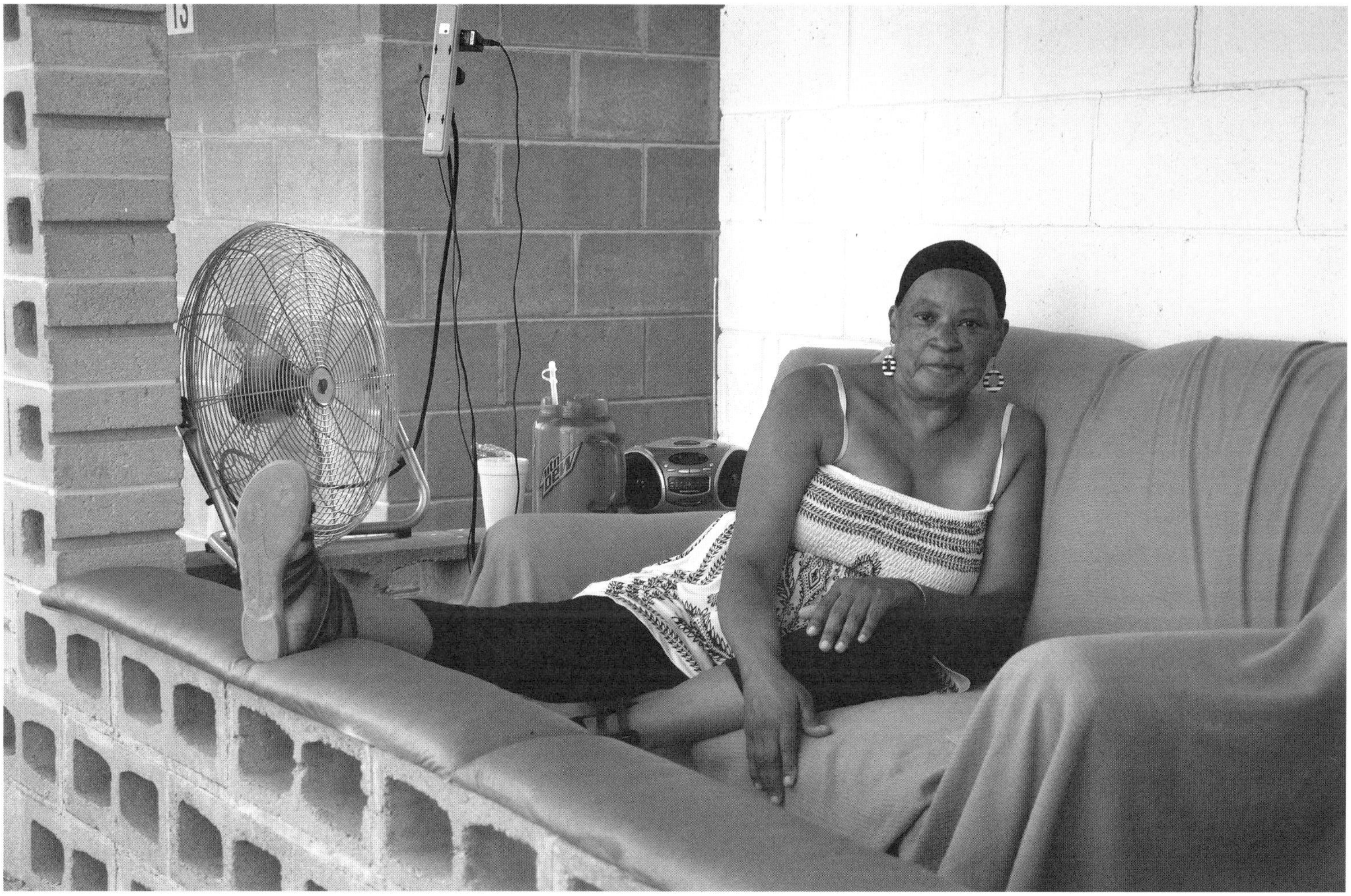

Born on the Grounds. Margaret Gaither Talford, Camp Welfare
Camp Meeting, 2014

Shirley and William Murphy built their tent in the spot where her mom's tent originally stood. Mount Carmel Camp Meeting, 2004

Mrs. Morine Jones says that she enjoys the preaching and the singing and just being with people. "I have been going to camp meeting ever since my mom was living. That was when I was nothing but a child. I am 86 years old. The Lord has blessed me because I have been going there for a long, long time." St. Paul Camp Meeting, October, 2006

Faydene Jones visits the tent of her classmate Roy Carr and they catch up on old times. For the past ten years the Rosenwald Class of 1958 celebrates their reunion on the grounds. McKenzie's Grove Camp Meeting, 2006

Arthur Gardner has built many of the stoves at St. Paul. He uniquely designs them to fit within a variety of kitchen spaces. He also builds stoves at Shady Grove and Indian Field camp meeting grounds. St. Paul Camp Meeting, 2014

Jelly cake at Tent #43, St. Paul Camp Meeting, 2014

Sam Pinckney remembers the stories that his grandparents use to tell him about camp meeting. Each year he cooks venison sausage at his family tent for breakfast. St. Paul Camp Meeting, 2007

Barbara Felder fries chicken inside the tent. A written menu which designates family responsibilities hangs in their family tent. St. Paul Camp Meeting, 2014

Carl Boyd enjoys cooking “drunk” chicken on his grill. He uses a variety of drink flavors including apple juice, orange juice, sodas, and wine. Shady Grove Camp Meeting, 2007

Gloria Jones fries chicken, fish, and french fries each year at her family's tent.
The Jones family has run a store at Shady Grove for the past 20 years.
Shady Grove Camp Meeting, 2013

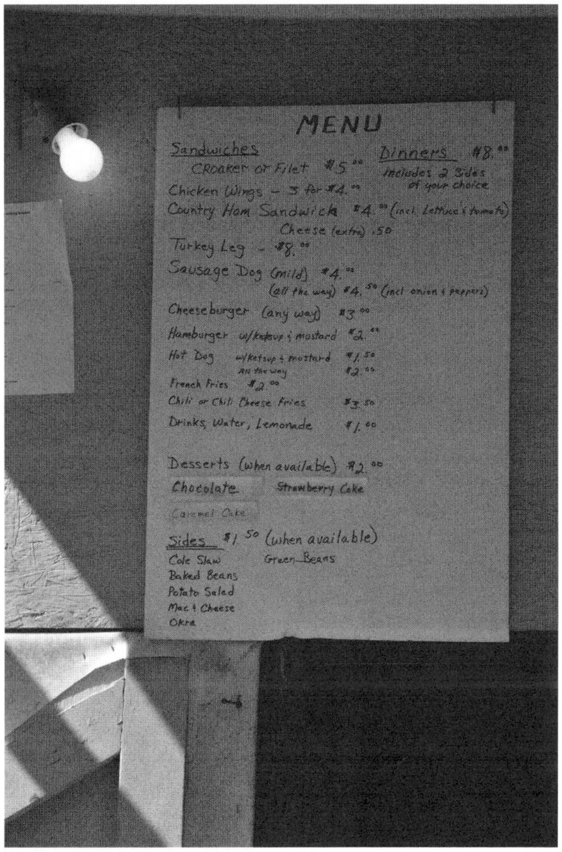

Concession Stand Menu, Tucker's Grove Camp Meeting, 2012

Kenneth Fish (left) and Joe Lewis Gabriel, Mott's Grove Camp Meeting, 2004

Camp Meeting Queen. Lennerd Mack, member of the board of trustees, and cousin, Mr. James Washington. Mrs. Mack moves into her tent at least two weeks before camp meeting begins. She is known to many people on the grounds as "The Camp Meeting Queen" St. Paul Camp Meeting, 2002

Music Stand. John Hull and cousin Paulette Hull Brown sell music CDs at McKenzie's Grove Camp meeting, 2005.

Photographer, Delar Winston, Mount Carmel Camp Meeting, 2010

Cooking Rutabagas, Barbara Washington, St. Paul Camp Meeting, 2014

4

Under the Arbor

Those who have experienced difficult challenges during the year come to camp meeting to ask for special blessings. Those who have already been blessed come to thank God. Many people come, too, with the desire to pay their blessings forward by helping others in need. Both yearning and gratitude are sometimes difficult to articulate without becoming emotional. This intimate exchange is welcome under the arbor, which is the literal and symbolic center of every campground.

THE ARBOR STRUCTURE

As already mentioned, early camp meetings were wild, woodsy affairs. But as the years passed, a more permanent structure for preaching, commonly referred to as the arbor or tabernacle, was erected. Certain internal elements are always present. The preacher's stand or pulpit is usually elevated from five to six and one-half feet above the ground. A mourner's bench was usually placed immediately in front of the stand. Camp participants who are seeking forgiveness and conversion are invited to sit there at a particular time in the service. The rest of the covered area consists of rows of wooden benches. The ceilings are high in the center, and the benches are generally low. Often older people will bring plump cushions so they can sit higher and more comfortably. Below the benches you will still see a freshly laid floor of straw, sand, or sawdust.

The lighting under the arbor is memorable, with naked bulbs hanging down and sometimes a bright stripe of fluorescence directly over the preacher's stand. At night their glow illuminates the old beams above, which have a special, antique smell that is stronger on rainy days. Wood smoke is another smell associated with the campground—in the fall it drifts in from the old drum or tank stoves in the tents.

The arbors used in the summer months usually have ceiling fans too. They make a light clicking sound as they wear over time, a bit like rain on an old tin roof. For anyone who grew up at camp meetings, it is a comforting sound highly reminiscent of childhood—a sound that still might tempt attendees to doze off on a hot summer day.

THE SCHEDULE

Although events vary from camp to camp, similar programming takes place over four to eight days, always ending on a Sunday. Some camp participants initiate camp services by marching around the arbor, singing traditional songs or blessing the grounds. The rest of the week consists of church services, which are varied by the many personalities involved and by the busloads of choirs and church groups that visit the campground in big waves. Services might start slowly on a Tuesday, Wednesday, and Thursday, with preachers and choirs that are younger or less well known. The crowd is smaller then, and the mood is still low-key. When more popular preachers and choirs step up on Friday and Saturday nights and on Sunday afternoon, the crowd swells enormously.

Historically the camp-meeting ground and arbor preceded the church. Today each campground is affiliated with several churches, so there are always plenty of preachers available. Most of the affiliated churches are located within or near the county in which the camp meeting is held. Guest preachers are still used to draw big crowds, just as in the old circuit-riding days. Unless the preacher comes from far away, church members and church choirs accompany their pastor in vans or large buses.

During the week services begin around 7:00 p.m., with adults working and children attending school during the day. (In fact the school bus used to pick children up and drop them off at Shady Grove.) On the weekend services begin earlier and consist of several preachers who each deliver a separate sermon. The larger campgrounds feature more pastors and offer more services throughout the week. Depending on the number of preachers, the time allotted for each one may vary.

"Big Sunday" is the final day of camp meeting, which always falls on that sacred day. People crowd the campground on the last weekend, and the final service is the culmination of the whole gathering.

Sunday morning usually begins with Bible study under the arbor. The service afterward is often led by the "host pastor," who has faithfully attended all the services throughout the week and introduced many of the other pastors. Usually his church is nearby—sometimes across the street. When they preach, their choir is showcased too.

During this service memorials are provided for any board of trustee members who have passed away since the last camp meeting. Participants are also recognized for making contributions of time or resources to the campground, and sometimes special appreciation is given to tent owners who had the most family members attend services throughout the week. After the Sunday service there is—of course—a great feast, with select tent owners hosting visiting preachers and their church families.

Mr. Shell Johnson, Shady Grove, 2004

Mr. William Bowman, Shady Grove, 2007

Shady Grove campground has a long history of using a trumpet-shaped horn to summon camp-goers to the arbor at designated times throughout the day. Caesar Wolfe, who founded Shady Grove after the Civil War, served as the first trumpeter. He passed the responsibility to his son, Marion "Mike" Wolfe, who passed it to his son, Richard Wolfe. Shell Johnson, who was born about 1903, was the next horn-blower to follow this tradition. A few years before Johnson's death, at age 106, his nephew William Bowman took over and has blown the horn ever since. One scholar who researched horn-blowing at Shady Grove suggested that the tradition could have existed at other campsites throughout the Southeast.[1]

"So it came about on the third day, when it was morning, that there were thunder and lightning flashes and a thick cloud upon the mountain and a very loud trumpet sound, so that all the people who were in the camp trembled. And Moses brought the people out of the camp to meet God, and they stood at the foot of the mountain."[2]

THE SERVICES

Certain unspoken rules are in place during services. Children are not to run or play around the arbor. Concession stands cannot serve customers through the front door (though some concession stand owners serve through a side door instead). Men respectfully remove their hats upon entering. If the person speaking is engaged in prayer, no one enters until they hear "amen."

Most services begin quietly, with just a small group seated up front and others gradually trickling in. As people assemble over the next thirty to forty minutes, a respected deacon or a trustee—often an older man—leads what is called the devotional service. That person always welcomes the congregation, reads a scripture, and offers a prayer. But the rest of the devotional service is freeform and based on audience participation.

With hardly a moment of silence between them, audience members stand up voluntarily to lead a spiritual and/or give a personal testimony. Occasionally they come up front, but usually they remain in place while someone brings them a microphone. Sometimes the person will describe a desperate situation and ask for prayer. More often they express gratitude to God for healing an illness, resolving a financial predicament, or keeping a loved one safe. When someone offers both a story and a spiritual, the meanings often dovetail in a beautiful way.

It is not unusual for someone singing or testifying to "get happy"—to feel the presence of God so powerfully that they dance in the aisle or even race gleefully around the outside of the arbor. When someone enters into a high level of spiritual ecstasy, male ushers or specially appointed "missionary women" surround them, fanning them and keeping them safe. The missionary women might, for example, lay a cloth on the ground and help a collapsing woman ease down gracefully. She is respectfully given the time she needs, then she returns to the congregation.

Whether people's behavior is subtle or dramatic, there is always a special feeling to a devotional service. Through song and story, people wring both tears and laughter from their fellow camp participants. They open a window into their most intimate experiences with God, revealing more of themselves than in any other public setting. Yet the process always feels comfortable and natural—like anything else that has brought people joy for many generations.

By the time the devotional service is finished, the crowd has fully assembled, and there is usually a certain electricity in the air. It is time for the preachers to preach and the choirs to shine, lifting both verbal and musical expression to a higher level.

Missionary Service, led by Reverend Glendora Sowell, Mount Carmel, 2011

Under the Arbor, Mott's Grove, 2006

Reverend Albert Perkins, Host Pastor, Tucker's Grove, 2009

New Arbor Dedication Prayer, St. Paul, 2011

Sunday Service, Reverend John Phifer, McKenzie's Grove, 2014

Reverend Willie Ray Derr, Sr, Tucker's Grove, 2014

Missionary March, Mount Carmel, 2007

Lester Lincoln, Shady Grove, 2012

Reverend Debra Parsons Carter, St. Paul, 2010

THE MUSIC

The music is always an impressive aspect of camp meeting. Among African Americans the traditional call-and-response format, with people singing without written lyrics in hand, continues to be practiced. Since most enslaved people could not read, there was no need for hymnals. They are not used at the seven camps that I have documented. Most of the camps, however, print a program that outlines each day of camp meeting. Occasionally the lyrics to a song will be printed in this program. (See Appendix C for a sample program.)

One change that has occurred in the music over time is that camp meetings now embrace the use of electric keyboards, drums, guitars, and other instruments. They are played softly during the devotional service, but the volume increases when it is time to back the choirs' big voices. When any music begins, hand clapping, foot stomping, and body swaying inevitably occur throughout the audience. The lyrics to a song once sung at Tucker's Grove are included here because they perfectly describe the experience.

The spiritual ecstasy that can overtake people during the devotional service may continue as the choirs sing and the preachers preach. The Spirit seems to hit people with special force when they are going through challenges, and there is cultural permission to express this through movement, through dance, and through vocal expression

IT'S SERVICE TIME!

When there's a praise in the temple, and a praise in the house
You can usher in the Spirit and remove the devil out
God will open up the window and the blessing He'll pour out
When there's a praise in the temple and a praise in the house
(repeat).

It's service time (echo) It's service time (echo)
Enter into the gate with thanksgiving and praise on your mind
It's service time (echo) It's service time (echo)
Get up out of that seat
Stand up on your feet
Let's clap to the beat
IT'S SERVICE TIME!!!! (REPEAT)

You won't leave like you came in Jesus' name
There's a blessing in this house you can claim
All you have to do is speak it—It's in your name
You won't leave like you came in Jesus' name!

It's service time (echo) It's service time (echo)
Enter into the gate with thanksgiving and praise on your mind
It's service time (echo) it's service time (echo)
Get up out of that seat
Stand up on your feet
Let's clap to the beat
IT'S SERVICE TIME!!![3]

that might seem strange to a newcomer. Nineteenth-century records of African American worship describe something extreme and barbaric, with people laughing, jerking, or barking like dogs.[4] You will not witness anything like that today. Did the historical records exaggerate? Or is contemporary behavior just more circumspect? Perhaps a little of both.

THE PREACHING

With the congregation spiritually stimulated by the choirs, there will be another prayer, and a collection is taken, accompanied by more singing. Then someone, often the host pastor, introduces the person who will preach. Each preacher has his or her own recognizable style of engaging the congregation. Each dresses distinctly, with some wearing robes, others wearing suits, and a few showing up in jeans. Most male preachers carry a handkerchief or towel to wipe away perspiration. All preachers use Bible quotes and personal stories to illustrate key points. Many ask questions and use repetitive statements to establish rapport with the congregation. At the height of the sermon, some preachers may energetically walk back and forth while maintaining eye contact with those seated around them. Some step down off the pulpit and interact directly with people, who at that point in the sermon are usually highly engaged.

One of the most powerful preachers I have ever had the privilege to hear is Rev. David Rice from the Great Falls area of South Carolina. Reverend Rice has preached at both Camp Welfare and Mount Carmel campgrounds for more than forty years. To hear an orator such as Reverend Rice is to experience the essence of the camp-meeting tradition. Preaching of this caliber can ignite in listeners a spiritual flame that consumes all sense of ego, allowing them to experience oneness with God and oneness with each other as well.

On one occasion, at the climax of a particularly powerful sermon, Reverend Rice shouted, "I am *through* here!" After several beats of silence, he slowly began to speak again. The congregation was ecstatic. He sat down several times, but they would not let him stop. In response to their applause, he popped up repeatedly to offer a few more words. As he threw his hands in the air, tossed the microphone from one hand to the other, and grabbed his Bible as if he were ready to leave, the congregation kept shouting out for *more*. Finally, when his sermon ended with a hoarse "May God bless you," the arbor exploded into intense applause.

THE ESSENCE OF THE TRADITION

People who have not personally experienced this kind of preaching might assume that it is theater or mass delusion or at the very least an exercise of ego on the part of the pastor. I would ask them to take a deeper look. African American camp meetings have always served the purpose of affirming humanity and helping people feel good about

Reverend David Rice, Mount Carmel, 2009

The following is an excerpt of a sermon preached in 2013 under the arbor:

You ought to be able to have a good time when you come to church. You ought not have a long face looking like you don't know what no one's talking about . . . You ought to sing and shout and you ought to know what you shouting about . . . Meeting is where they clap their hands . . . and move around and . . . oh lord . . . *shout* with joy . . . *shout* with everything you got!

Oh . . . lord . . . I want to sit down here. Anybody got to go to the meeting . . . Anybody have you made up in your mind that you want to go to the meeting . . . Meeting! Ah . . . oh Lord . . . Meeting! Ah . . . in my Father's house . . . Meeting! Ah . . . I'm through here. . . Ohhh . . . I sing because I'm happy, I sing because I'm free. The eye on the sparrow . . . ha. I know . . . ohhh . . . meeting! (He sits down, then jumps back up.)

Anybody here . . . *ha.* Meeting . . . ha. I'm through . . . (He looks around at the congregation.) I'm through . . . Meeting. I wonder if you are going . . . Are you going? You can't go with your hands folded. You got to . . . you . . .ohhh. I'm through here. I'm through here.

Meeting . . . ha. Meeting . . . ha. Ohhh yeah . . . meeting on the ole . . . God bless you. God keep you. Ohhh . . . ohhh . . . I know . . . our Redeemer lives because He lives in me . . . Ohhh ha . . . (He sits down, then jumps up, throws both hands in the air, and grabs his Bible.)

Ohhh . . . Shout hallelujah . . . Hallelujah . . . I'm through. I'm through. I'm through. I give praise to the omnipotent. Ohh, to the one who got all power.

Will you be there? Let me ask you a question . . . will you be there? *Yeahhhhh* . . . (He points the microphone at the congregation.) Meeting around God's throne . . . May God bless you . . . (He sits down.) Rev. David Rice, Mount Carmel campground, September 7, 2013.

themselves in a world where racism and the history of slavery affect them on a daily basis. Despite the many improvements in African American life over the last decades, that same purpose is still fulfilled today.

Also a deeper and more universal purpose is served by our best preachers. For those who are open to such an experience, the sermon becomes a captivating song. Then it becomes an embrace. Finally it feels like a mighty ship that sails the whole congregation across the dark channel of daily emotions—fear, anger, loneliness, and suffering of all kinds—into a vivid awareness of the presence and power of God.

This shift of consciousness is not unique to camp meetings or even to Christianity. It transcends religious boundaries. Sometimes it is felt, too, by people who do not even call themselves religious. People who experience this vivid and direct connection with the divine are called mystics. This word is often associated with solitude, renunciation, and severe trials. But anyone who attends a testimony meeting realizes that solitude, renunciation, and severe trials are not just for monks who sit on top of mountains. They are part of every spiritual journey.

Through the songs and stories of our fellow travelers and through the oratory of our most powerful preachers, camp meetings help us find untold rewards in "the wilderness and the solitary place." They make our "desert . . . rejoice, and blossom as the rose."[5] Camp meetings, in other words, make mystics of us all.

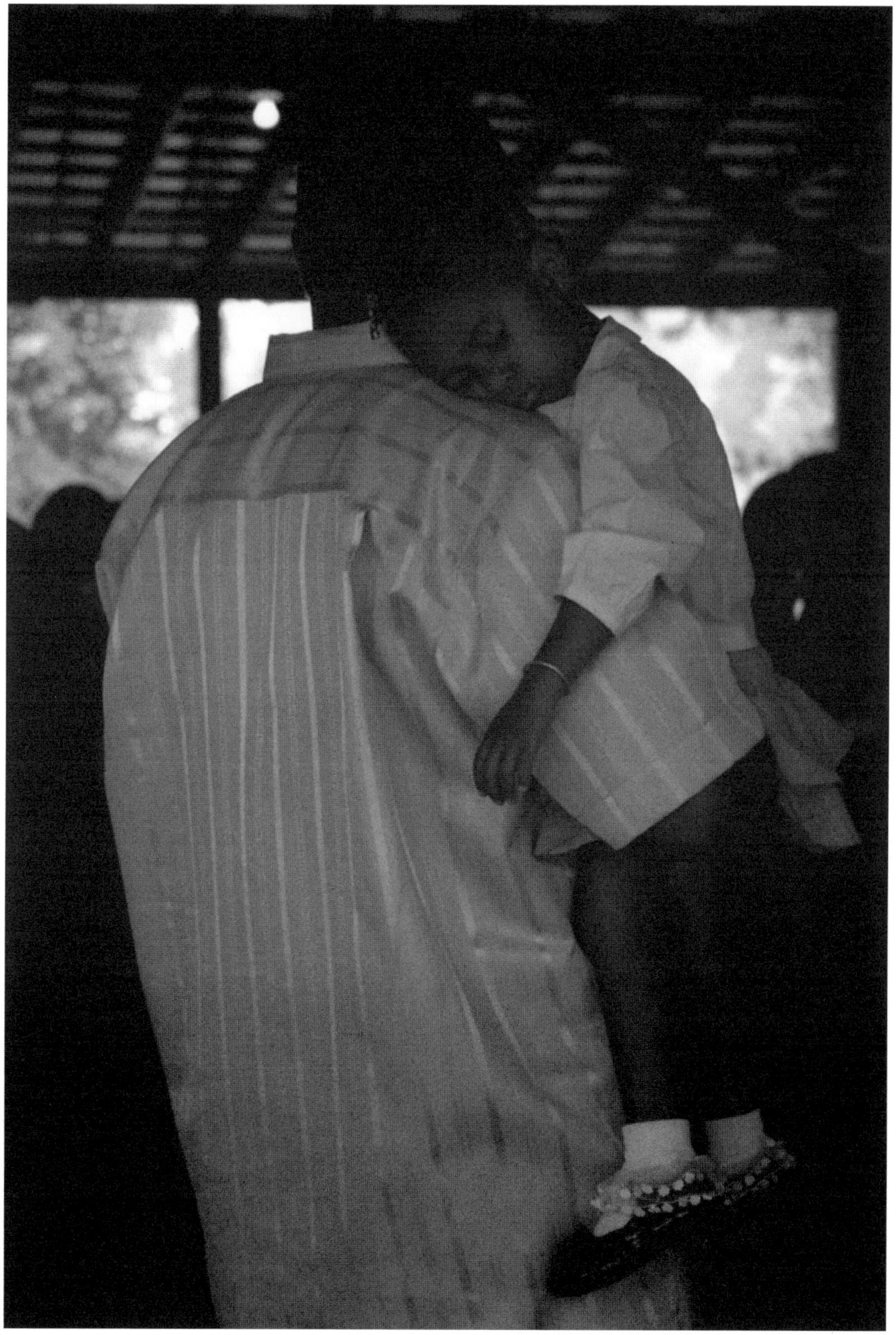

Young man with Child, McKenzie's Grove, 2006

Prayer service led by Reverend Otis Scott, Shady Grove, 2012

Offering, Alfred Calvin, chair board of trustees and guest pastor. St. Paul, 2014

Choir, Mount Carmel, 2006

Alin Rigby participates in fellowship under the arbor at Shady Grove Camp ground, 2014. She is a descendent of Caesar Wolfe, founder of the campgrounds.

Awards Ceremony led by Jerome Jones, Chair, Board of Trustees,
Shady Grove, 2012

Reverend Eugene Collins, St. Paul, 2006

Shirley Brown and her son Ryan leading a song under the arbor. St. Paul, 2012

5

The Next Generation

Young children are nurtured into camp meeting from the day they are born. Babies are proudly shown off, passed from person to person, and smothered with hugs and kisses. Older children wander freely around the campground's circular design, which allows them to remain under watchful eyes at all times. From a child's point of view, the campground is a larger-than-life communal space filled with kinfolk. What begins with the love of family extends into dozens of strong, semifamilial relationships and then eventually grows into a lifelong bond with the whole camp-meeting tradition.

CAMP ACTIVITIES FOR CHILDREN

Most campgrounds are cognizant of the fact that children need to be involved in their own special activities. Organizing these activities is sometimes quite challenging. Both Saint Paul and Shady Grove have Saturday morning children's programs that take place during camp meeting. The program at Shady Grove includes a health fair as well as guest speakers who discuss topics relevant to youth. Children can also win bicycles and other prizes and are invited to a special meal consisting of hamburgers, hot dogs, and other treats.

In addition to scheduled activities, children are free to socialize and meet new friends on the grounds. Although some families have televisions in their tents, most children prefer to stay outside. They have a wide-open space in which to run and play, and there is so much excitement outside that they are quickly drawn into it.

Children also do not spend a lot of time talking on cell phones or playing with technology on the campgrounds. Younger children toss balls, play tag, run, jump, and play in the dirt. They make mud pies and scoop dirt up into cups, almost as if they were at the beach. They throw pinecones and build sculptures from sticks they find on the ground. They turn cartwheels and play some of the games that were a familiar part of my own childhood. Older children socialize and tease one other, and everyone enjoys the feeling of kinship that spontaneously takes place in nature.

Often you will see young children with friends or pushing babies in strollers as they walk around the interior and exterior circle of the grounds. There is a certain level of trust involved when a parent or family member gives a child this responsibility. As children circle the grounds, however, they will always run into adults who know them or are related to them.

Narrow spaces,
Mott's Grove, 2005

Favorite activities, Mott's Grove, 2004

Children on grounds, Camp Welfare, 2010

Usually parents and children establish rules before they come to the campgrounds. Younger children know to check in with their parents at designated times throughout the day. Most children have evening curfews and know when to return to their tents. As the evening sky turns to dusk, most young children start making their way back to the family tent. My sister-in-law, Debra Byers, describes her memories of going down to home of Red Smith, who owned a jukebox and lived in a house on the backside of the grounds. She exclaimed that "he would put the jukebox outside, and we would go down to his house to socialize, dance, and listen to music. We spent the entire week on the campgrounds and had to go to the arbor service. After service, we would go to the jukebox and would be there all night long if we could. My daddy sent my brother to come get us. He suspected that we were down there."[1]

On the weekends the campgrounds can become very crowded. Then children know that they have to be careful not to get lost, and many stick closer to their families.

GROWING INTO THE TRADITION

At camp meeting family memories invariably bubble to the surface. Children hear funny stories about incidents that happened to their parents on the grounds. They hear stories with messages about human folly and wisdom. They hear conversations about relatives who have passed away. Some families display a collage of photographs in their tents showcasing generations of family members. And as children walk the grounds, they are often asked whom they are related to or are recognized because they resemble a parent or grandparent.

No one plans to come to camp meeting to teach family history to the children. That link to the past is forged naturally, the same way children learn values through the day-to-day activity of living with their elders. Just as children learn their own family history, they also learn about the tradition of camp meeting. As rules, rituals, and procedures are modeled for them, the tradition becomes engrained. Even if they go away to college or move far away, the strong imprint of bonds to family, friends, and community will carry many of them back to the grounds each year. And their reason for coming home may be just as much related to camp meeting as it is to their own family. Calendars are marked with this important date far in advance. Family reunions are often scheduled around it and held on the grounds. For those of us raised in this tradition, then, the boundary between family and camp meeting gets blurred from the time we are very small.

Pearline Brown Glass, Shady Grove, 2007

Kelsey McCleave, Mott's Grove, 2005

Presiding Elder Alfred Carson and family, McKenzie's Grove, 2006

Bynum Family Tent, Tucker's Grove, 2014 "When we were young, we would move out here on Friday and stay until the next Friday. I remember we use to go to the dance hall and play the piccolo. It was located at Mrs. Zettie's house."

Toilets, St. Paul, 2014

ZyRiah Woodard (left) and Jy Crawford wash dishes at the outdoor faucet, Camp Welfare, 2011

The Neal Family Birthday Celebration, St. Paul, 2013

Cora Potts, St. Paul, 2006

Former Student, McKenzie's Grove, 2012

THEN AND NOW

Though one of the great joys of camp meeting is this vivid link to our personal and collective past, it is only fair to mention certain ways in which modern life can dilute the experience for some people who attend.

In the distant past, for example, people stayed on the grounds until camp meeting ended. Now people can drive out to the grounds, then quickly return home. They do not necessarily spend the night, and they may not spend more than a few hours. So for some, camp meeting does not involve the same commitment that it did in decades past. Nor does the experience necessarily build to the same intensity.

Reflecting new modes of transportation and diverse job opportunities far beyond farming, camp-meeting schedules have changed. Historically sermons and Bible studies were provided throughout the day. Those frequent opportunities to study the Bible provided greater spiritual focus for children. Now Bible study occurs primarily on Sunday morning prior to the service, and the number of children in attendance is minimal.

Another noticeable change is the behavior of children during services, which some preachers mention chidingly during their sermons. As children we had no choice but to sit quietly and listen, picking up whatever insights we might grasp. The only permissible lapse in attention was to doze off on a hot day.

Today some children are clearly distracted under the arbor. And some never enter the arbor at all, running and playing outside while their parents attend the service. Once a little boy engaged in a game dashed right through the arbor, oblivious to the preaching.

Moreover some adults no longer enter the arbor. They socialize outside, enjoying camp meeting with family and friends. This may not be obvious during the week. But when the weekend crowds arrive, perhaps as many as half the adults never attend a service. They focus exclusively on the activities taking place around the perimeter of the grounds.

Comments from these casual visitors indicate how unaware they are about the camp-meeting tradition. One enthusiastic entrepreneur told me, "I'm going to go home and start a festival just like this!" I resisted the urge to say, "This is not a festival. We are not here to make money." Another person listed a dozen practical uses for the campground during the off-season, exclaiming, "What a waste of a space!" Again I resisted the urge to get her up to speed on the concept of hallowed ground.

Another cause for concern is behavior that is radically out of sync with the spirit of camp meeting. Once I saw two boys playing. The smaller of the two initially enjoyed the roughhousing, then changed his mind and ran to complain to his mother. Blasting across the campground, her eyes lit with fear and rage, she dealt the other child a verbal blow far more severe than I could ever imagine. Thinking of Jesus's statement "Blessed are the peacemakers,"[2] I could only shake my head. Fear and rage are two of the emotions that we unlearn under the arbor, through our immersion in nature and through our best camp-meeting encounters with family and friends.

These incidents represent a tendency that raises concerns for many people who love camp meeting. No one believes that these popular historical events will end. But many wonder if the tradition is being undermined in more subtle ways. The question is always: What can we do, individually and collectively, to help camp meetings maintain their spiritual integrity?

IN THE SPIRIT OF THE ANCESTORS

Spiritual integrity is still what draws many thousands of people to camp meetings each year. There is something profound about setting aside that sacred time far in advance. Something profound about being in nature and gathering under the oak or pine trees. And something profound about choosing to step back in time—to minimal plumbing, worn or mismatched furniture, and no way to avoid the ubiquitous dirt and dust.

Though not everyone goes under the arbor, they can still hear the sounds of singing and preachers' preaching far across the grounds. There is always an opportunity for both children and adults to mature and find their sustenance at the center instead of the periphery. The late Deacon Isaiah Springs, chair of McKenzie's Grove said, "When I was younger, I loved walking the grounds and holding hands with the girls. Now, it's all about the service." Springs also said, "In the early 1920s, my great-grandfather was chair of the board. He often told me that one of these days that I'd be walking in his footsteps. Back then I said, 'No way!'"[3]

Only time will tell if today's children will return to camp meetings hungry for spiritual sustenance, eventually taking on the leadership roles that their parents and grandparents occupy today. Because of the foundation laid in each child, one can only hope that the celebration and significance of camp meeting will continue to follow the pattern put in place more than a century ago when the grounds were first designated as places for religious worship.

What makes thousands of people return to camp meeting each year? Patricia Charthern, retired elementary school principal and descendant of Caesar Wolfe at Shady Grove camp meeting, said that "it's just in our DNA!" Others proclaim that it is about family and ancestors. Bertha Gladden, a camp participant from Camp Welfare, proclaimed that she is doing it to keep the memory and legacy of her ancestors alive. She exclaimed that "the younger generation will have to keep it going so that their families will not be forgotten." Shirley Kennedy, also a lifelong participant at Camp Welfare, said, "I am seventy-one years old, and it is all I have ever known."[4] When you grow up attending camp meeting, you expect that it is something that everyone participates in. As for me, I continue to imagine the ancestors who left their footprints there and the hard work, determination, sweat, and tears of thousands of people who made camp meeting what it is today. Many have sung, have laughed, have cried, have repented their sins, and have poured out their testimonies during both good and bad years. Many have left the grounds spiritually fulfilled and have journeyed back home committed to a new level of love, joy, and service in their personal endeavors. I look forward to attending camp meeting. The people that I meet and their stories continue to inspire me. I love the preaching, the singing, reconnecting with old friends, and meeting new ones. My parents introduced me to a unique and heartwarming religious tradition. They thought it was important for us to attend. A few years ago, a preacher at Camp Welfare described my own feelings exactly: "I can feel the spirits of those who were here years ago," she told the congregation. "I can still feel the exhilaration."[5]

Zula and Isaiah Springs, McKenzie's Grove, 2014

Isaiah Springs, McKenzie's Grove, 2014

John Miller, Jr. and daughter, Abigail, 2005

Ah'Zion Parsons, Motts Grove, 2014

Reunion, Harriett Gabriel and great-granddaughter Victoria, Mott's Grove, 2013

Randy Ross and daughter, Raven, Mott's Grove 2005

Conclusion

After fifteen years of making an annual journey to seven camp-meeting grounds, I am as motivated to attend today as I was back in 1996. Since that time I have met so many wonderful new family and friends, too many to count! What a blessing it has been for me to be able to meet so many caring individuals, who upon our initial meeting did not know me. How important it was for me to capture the voices, faces, and stories that have a long history with the campgrounds. Everyone welcomed me with opened arms. They trusted me enough to provide me with their personal camp-meeting stories, invited me into their tent or shared delicious home-cooked meals with me, and escorted me to the tents of their family and friends. They so graciously discussed their own histories with the grounds. I have been invited to family reunions in New York and birthday parties for elders, who celebrated eighty-five, ninety, and one hundred years on earth. On a sadder note, I receive phone calls informing me that someone from the campgrounds has passed away. I am contacted when important events take place on the campgrounds—the Martin Luther King Jr. parade at Shady Grove, Friends and Family Day at Tucker's Grove, the Rosenwald Class of 1958 reunion at McKenzie's Grove, and the dedication of historic markers at Camp Welfare, Saint Paul, and Shady Grove. What a witness to history in the making!

Camp meeting is engrained in my heart and soul. It was a history that was waiting for me to tell through my own lens and my family story, through my friends and camp participants. I am honored to have grown up in camp meeting and to have an opportunity to witness history as it continues to unfold. Camp meetings are a place where the past meets the present day. They are a significant historical and living tradition that continues to unfold, a phenomenon that, in my opinion, will always be a unique place to worship.

APPENDIX A

BACKGROUND INFORMATION

CAMP WELFARE (1876)—FAIRFIELD COUNTY, SOUTH CAROLINA

Camp Welfare, founded shortly after the Civil War by the African Methodist Episcopal (AME) Church, is located in an isolated area in northeastern Fairfield County. The site consists of ten to eleven acres of permanent and semipermanent "tents" lined up in rows, as well as an open-air arbor. The local AME Zion church, which sits on the grounds, was built in the 1930s to provide shelter for year-round church meetings. In addition there are two permanent wooden concession stands on the grounds—one more than one hundred years old—and several portable concession stands as well. A cemetery is located on the backside of the grounds. Years ago an early twentieth-century one-room schoolhouse stood on the grounds. It was used by neighborhood children until it closed in 1955. Camp Welfare was placed on the National Register of Historic Places in 1984. The historic marker was unveiled in 2003.[1]

MCKENZIE'S GROVE (1875)—CATAWBA COUNTY, NORTH CAROLINA

McKenzie's Grove was established a decade after the Civil War, when landowner Robert McKenzie sold five and one-half acres to worshippers for twenty-two dollars. It was founded by the AME Zion church. Later, at some hazy point in the campground's history, a road was built directly through the middle of it. According to local legend, when a corn farmer was asked if authorities could direct the road through his land, he said no. Campground worshippers were apparently not offered the same choice, so the road was built through theirs, separating some of the tents from the rest of the campground. There are nineteen tents at McKenzie's Grove and also a cemetery. In 1975 the aging arbor was rebuilt and rededicated. Churches of various denominations surround the campground and are affiliated with it. They include Smyres Chapel, Providence United Methodist, Browns Chapel, and Liberty Hill Baptist.[2]

MOUNT CARMEL (1866)—LANCASTER COUNTY, SOUTH CAROLINA

Mount Carmel AME Zion Church and the campground associated with it were founded in 1866 by Isom Caleb Clinton (1830–1904), a former slave. The following year, 1867, the South Carolina conference of the AME Zion Church was organized, and Clinton was ordained a deacon. He was an important leader in the state and later became bishop. Clinton's younger brother, Frederick Albert Clinton (1834–1890), was also instrumental in the growth of Mount Carmel. There are more than one hundred tents and dozens of camper trailers on the grounds, along with an open-sided arbor, a church, a concession-stand area, and a cemetery. In 2002 a "street dedication service" was held. The streets, named mainly for emergencies, include Camper Place, Holy Ghost Headquarters, Arbor Square, Concession Boulevard, and Cemetery Lane.[3]

MOTT'S GROVE (1872)—CATAWBA COUNTY, NORTH CAROLINA

Another campground founded shortly after the Civil War, Mott's Grove was named after Dr. John Mott, who came upon a group of his African American neighbors having a workshop service one evening. Mott, a leader of the Republic party, donated nine acres for the purpose of spiritual meetings. The campground was founded by the AME congregations and based on the doctrines of the AME and AME Zion Church. Many of the people who attended Mott's Grove had attended Ball's Creek camp meeting with their slave owners before the war. At Mott's Grove today twenty-eight tents surround the open-sided arbor. Motts Grove United Methodist Church is located beside the campground, and a cemetery sits behind the church. Years ago Mott's Grove had so many tents that they had to start a second row of them on the grounds. Over the years vandalism, fires, and storms reduced the number of tents. There is a cement-block concession stand and several portable concession stands near the main road.[4]

SHADY GROVE (1870)—DORCHESTER COUNTY, SOUTH CAROLINA

According to local tradition, Caesar Wolfe, a former slave, started Shady Grove shortly after the Civil War. Wolfe persuaded other former slaves to help a rice farmer gather his crop before it was destroyed by an approaching storm. To express his appreciation, the farmer, S. M. Knight, informally gave them the land to be used exclusively for religious purposes. The land was later deeded to the former slaves. There are 133 tents on the grounds. The arbor, which has been renovated many times, stands in the middle. At Shady Grove concession stands are built into some of the tents. Shady

Grove participants love to say that the annual meeting has never been canceled, except during a nationwide influenza outbreak in 1912. Shady Grove United Methodist Church is located off the Charleston Highway in Saint George. The Caesar Wolfe Historical Center was built in 2008 and dedicated on October 25, 2008. The historic marker was dedicated on October 18, 2010.[5]

SAINT PAUL CAMPGROUND (1880)—DORCHESTER COUNTY, SOUTH CAROLINA

Fifteen years after the Civil War, the Trustees of Saint Paul AME Church purchased land for a campground. According to courthouse records, under the Reverend Joseph White, trustees Caesar Dunning, W. A. Heyward, Isaac Lincoln, and William Hutson paid $210.00 for 113 acres. Most of this land still belongs to the church, which stands on the southwest side of the parcel. A few small sections have been deeded to members of the community for house sites. There are sixty-nine tents on the grounds. Concession stands are built into the front of six of these tents. The property south of Saint Paul is farmed. Several affiliated churches in nearby towns—Harleyville, Saint George, Ridgeville, and Dorchester—share preachers and choirs, and their members tent at Saint Paul. The marker showing National Register status was dedicated in 2011.[6]

TUCKER'S GROVE, 1874—LINCOLN COUNTY, NORTH CAROLINA

Tucker's Grove campground consists of seven acres purchased from William C. Tucker after the Civil War. Additional land has been purchased in recent years. There are one hundred tents on the grounds with an open-sided arbor and a large concession-stand area located on the front side of the grounds. Tucker's Grove United Methodist Church and cemetery are located directly across the road from the campground. Funding from the Duke Endowment was used to make major repairs to the arbor in 2016 and was completed in 2017. The rededication service took place on the final Sunday of camp meeting, August 2017. A stone monument made of granite erected outside the arbor, bears the inscription *Tucker's Grove Campground, 1874*, and has an image of a cross on the other side. It was dedicated in 2002. Five United Methodist churches—Brevard, Ebenezer, Rock Hill, Saint James, and Tucker's Grove—Gold Hill Baptist Church sponsor the campground. Tucker's Grove was placed on the National Register of Historic Places in 1972, more than one hundred years after the campground was established.[7]

APPENDIX B

AN EXAMPLE OF CAMP MEETING RULES AND PROCEDURES

SHADY GROVE

Ground Rules and Operating Procedures for Tent Holders

- Any person desiring a location for a tent must obtain permission from the Board of Trustees.
- Persons who build a tent on the premises will not have a deed and title to the property. Tents may only be transferred with the consent of the Trustees and the tent holder. Any dispute over the ownership of the tent shall be adjudicated by the Board of Trustees.
- Each tent holder is responsible for and will pay such amounts as assessed yearly by the Board of Trustees for the upkeep of the Campground.
- Each tent holder is responsible for the conduct of those living in or visiting his or her tent site. Disorderly conduct, i.e., cursing, fighting, playing loud music, etc. . . . are grounds for sanction. Repeated violation of this rule may be grounds for the Board of Trustees to review and make a determination as to the continued occupancy of the tent.
- No selling of any kind will be allowed on the grounds or within a mile of the grounds without permission from the Board of Trustees. All stores and other establishments will pay such amount as assessed yearly by the Board of Trustees. All stores and other establishments must be closed during worship periods. The sale of whips, firecrackers, toy pistols, and other such items will result in the immediate revocation of permission to sell and operate a store or some site established.
- Drinking or selling alcoholic beverages on the grounds is expressly forbidden. Violation of this rule will be grounds for the tent spot to be taken from the tent holder. In the event the tent spot is taken, it will revert to the Board of Trustees.
- Ball playing on the grounds is not allowed. Balls or other such sporting equipment may be confiscated at the discretion of the Chief of Secretary, Security Team

Member, or any Trustee. Boom boxes and/or musical devices being operated in violation of the loud noise rule may also be confiscated.

- Tent holders are responsible for all children and youth living in or visiting their tents. Security will notify the parents of children or youth exhibiting unruly or disobedient behavior. Repeated or continued unruliness of the children or young may be grounds for the Board of Trustees to review and make a determination as to the continued occupancy of the tent.
- The Board of Trustees will inspect all tents each year in order to notify tent holders if repairs to their respective tents are needed. Tents can be no more than twelve (12) feet in width. If tents must be rebuilt, the trustees strongly recommend using wood. This is recommended in order to preserve the cultural and historical aspects of the Campground.
- Dorchester County provides garbage pick up every morning during camp meeting. Tent holders must properly bag their garbage and place all garbage at the rear of the tent. Garbage will not be picked up if not properly bagged.
- Tent holders with tents on the southwest side of the campground will have two (2) parking spaces directed behind their respective tents. All other tent holders and visitors must park in the designated spaces.
- Access to the inside of the grounds during worship services are limited to emergencies and/or extreme necessity as determined by the Board of Trustees. Tent holders and visitors are strongly encouraged to use the rear entrances during worship periods.
- Barbecue grills on wheels are prohibited on the grounds. Tent holders may use small freestanding grills at the rear behind a tent.
- To all tent holders there will be no wood or debris left behind the tent before or after camp meeting.
- During worship service there will be no walking or standing around the inside grounds unless going to or from worship service.
- The Chief of Security and Security Team, along with the Board of Trustees are responsible for enforcing ground rules and operating procedures.

APPENDIX C

CAMP MEETING PROGRAM

Sunday, October 12, 2014—Annual Gospelfest–3:30 p.m.
October 13, 2014–October 18, 2014 7:30 P.M.
Nightly & October 19, 2014 10:30 A.M. & 3:00 P.M.

Elder Charles Frazier, Presiding

✦ Monday, October 13, 2014

SPEAKER Rev. James Albert Ross,
Wesley United Methodist Church, Beaufort, SC

SPEAKER Rev. Jimmy Washington,
Red Bank & Bethel U.M. Churches, Smoaks, SC/Walterboro, SC

✦ Tuesday, October 14, 2014

SPEAKER Rev. George Felder,
New Hope A.M.E. Church, St. George, SC

SPEAKER Rev. Reverdy Capers, Sr.,
Good Hope Baptist Church, St. George, SC

✦ Wednesday, October 15, 2014

SPEAKER Rev. Charles K. Wilson,
New Grace U.M. Church, St. George, SC

SPEAKER Rev. Audrey Boozer,
Harleyville Parish (Morris Chapel/St. Daniels U.M. Churches)

✦ Thursday, October 16, 2014

SPEAKER Rev. George Goodwin,
St. John Missionary Baptist Church, Ridgeville, SC

SPEAKER Rev. Priscilla Lambright,
Lovely Hill Baptist Church, Holly Hill, SC

✦ Friday, October 17, 2014

SPEAKER Rev. Carol Berry,
New Mt. Zion AME Church, Harleyville, SC

SPEAKER Rev. John T. Miller,
Emanuel Baptist Church, Summerville, SC

✦ Saturday, October 18, 2014

3 P.M.–5 P.M.: Youth Hour "Fun Day for all age" Sis. Kim Ling, Coordinator
"DJJ Presenters"

✦ Saturday Evening: 7:30 P.M.

Speaker Rev. Charles Ryans, Associate Minister of House of God, Five Mile, Charleston, SC

Speaker Bishop David Baxter, True Light Sound of Praise, Myrtle Beach, SC

✦ Sunday, October 19, 2014

10:30 A.M. Sunday School	Bro. Solomon Berry, Superintendent Teachers: Sis. Zeddie Boyd & Others
11:30 A.M.	Rev. Henry Gabe, III Greater St. Paul AME Church, Dorchester, SC
12:30 P.M.–2:30 P.M.	Lunch
3:00 P.M.	Rev. Francis McPhearson, Bethal AME Church, McClellanville, SC
3:30 P.M.	Rev. Mark Mitchell, St. John & Oak Grove U.M. Churches
4:00 P.M.	Rev. John Smalls, Bethal AME Church, St. George, SC
4:30 P.M.	Tr. Elder Eugene Davis, House of God, Harleyville, SC
5:00 P.M.	Rev. H. T. Gainey, Edisto Fork U.M. Church, Orangeburg, SC

NOTES

CHAPTER 1 MY STORY

1. Proverbs 22:6 (NET).

CHAPTER 2 BACK THEN

1. Bruce, *And They All Sang Hallelujah*, 54.
2. Johnson, *Frontier Camp Meeting*, 25.
3. Beougher, "Camp Meetings and Circuit Riders," 1.
4. Goetz, "Christianity on the Early American Frontier," 29.
5. Webb, "Introducing Black Harry Hoosier."
6. Johnson, *Frontier Camp Meeting*, 114.
7. Ibid., xiii.
8. Margaret Gaither-Talford, interview with the author, August 22, 2014.
9. Marjorie McClinton McMurray, interview with the author, August 15, 2001.
10. McDonald, "Hornblower's Playing Is of Historical Note."

CHAPTER 3 CAMP LIFE

1. Smith, Kenneth, Pastor at Pineville and St. Stephens United Methodist Church, 2005.

CHAPTER 4 UNDER THE ARBOR

1. Kridel, "Gabriel in Black Paradise," 263.
2. Exodus 19:16–17 (NIV).
3. Dorothy Norwood. "It's Service Time." Elyrics.net, http://www.elyrics.net/read/d/dorothy-norwood-lyrics/it_s-service-time-(praise-in-the-temple)-lyrics.html (accessed May 21, 2105).
4. Johnson, *Frontier Camp Meeting*, 146.
5. Isaiah 35:1 (KJV).

CHAPTER 5 THE NEXT GENERATION

1. Debra Byers, interview with the author, September 27, 2015.
2. Matthew 5:9 (KJV).
3. Isaiah Springs, interview with the author, October 14, 2014.
4. Patricia Charthern, interview with the author, October 24, 2015; Bertha Gladden, interview with the author, August 21, 2015; Shirley Kennedy, interview with the author, August 21, 2015.
5. Reverend Cynthia Perry Camp Welfare, African Methodist Episcopal Zion Church, August, 20, 2003.

APPENDIX A

1. "Historic Camp Welfare," US Department of the Interior, Heritage Conservation and Recreation Service, National Register of Historic Places Inventory, Nomination Form, http://www.nationalregister.sc.gov/fairfield/S10817720006/S10817720006.pdf (accessed May 26, 2015); Malvina Moore, interview with the author, August 24, 2001.
2. "Historic and Architectural Resources of Catawba County, NC," US Department of the Interior, National Park Service, Multiple Property Documentation Form, dfhost.focus.nps.gov/docs/NRHP/Text/64500352.pdf (accessed May 24, 2015); McKenzie's Grove program booklet (1972); Isaiah Springs, interview with the author, October 14, 2014.
3. "Mount Carmel A.M.E. Zion Campground," US Department of the Interior, National Park Service, National Register of Historic Places Inventory—Nomination Form, http://www.nationalregister.sc.gov/lancaster/S10817729007/S10817729007.pdf (accessed May 26, 2015); "A Souvenir of Sovereignty: A Collection of Pictorial and Updated Events of Mt Carmel Camp Meeting." Willing Workers–Mount Carmel AME Zion Church (2006).
4. "Historic and Architectural Resources of Catawba County, NC," US Department of the Interior, National Park Service, Multiple Property Documentation Form, dfhost.focus.nps.gov/docs/NRHP/Text/64500352.pdf (accessed May 24, 2015); Linda Fish, interview with the author, April 16, 2015.
5. Alin Rigby, interview with the author, October 20, 2002.
6. "St. Paul Campground," US Department of the Interior, National Park Service, National Register of Historic Places Registration Form, http://www.nationalregister.sc.gov/dorchester/S10817718008/S10817718008.pdf (accessed May 26, 2015); Alfred Calvin, interview with the author, May 21, 2015; Herbert Gardner, interview with the author, May 5, 2015.
7. "Tucker's Grove Camp Meeting Ground," United States Department of the Interior, National Park Service, National Register of Historic Places Inventory—Nomination Form, www.hpo.ncdcr.gov/nr/LN0011.pdf (accessed May 25, 2015).

BIBLIOGRAPHY

Beougher, Timothy K. "Camp Meetings and Circuit Riders: Did You Know? Little-Known and Remarkable Facts about Camp Meetings and Circuit Riders." *Christianity Today,* January 1, 1995, 2–3, http://www.christianitytoday.com/ch/1995/issue45/4502.html.Bruce, Dickson D., Jr. *And They All Sang Hallelujah: Plain-Folk Camp-Meeting Religion, 1800–1845.* Knoxville: University of Tennessee Press, 1974.

Goetz, David L. "Christianity on the Early American Frontier: A Gallery of Trendsetters in the Religious Wilderness." *Christianity Today,* January 1, 1995, 26–29, http://www.christianitytoday.com/ch/1995/issue45/4526.html.

Johnson, Charles A. *The Frontier Camp Meeting: Religion's Harvest Time.* Dallas: Southern Methodist University Press, 1955.

Kridel, Craig. "Gabriel in Black Paradise." In *Perspectives in Brass Scholarship: Proceedings of the International Historic Brass Symposium,* edited by Stewart Arlen Carter, 263–70. Hillsdale, NY: Pendragon, 1998.

McDonald, Bill. "Hornblower's Playing Is of Historical Note." *Dorchester County (SC) Eagle Record,* August 1, 1991.

Webb, Stephen H. "Introducing Black Harry Hoosier: The History behind Indiana's Namesake." *Indiana Magazine of History* 98, no. 1 (March 2002): 30–41, http://scholarworks.iu.edu/journals/index.php/imh/article/view/11895/17497.